CHOOSING RIGHT

How to Find God's Will when Choosing a Marriage Partner

by Jayce Tohline

All scripture quotations, unless otherwise noted, are taken from The New King James Version, Copyright 1982 by Thomas Nelson, Inc. Used by permission. All rights reserved.

Scripture quotations marked "Amplified" are taken from The Amplified Bible - The Amplified Old Testament copyright 1965, 1987 by Zondervan Corporation, Grand Rapids, Michigan. New Testament copyright 1958, 1987 by The Lockman Foundation, La Habra, California. Used by permission.

Scripture quotations marked "KJV" are taken from the King James Version.

Choosing Right – How to Find God's Will when Choosing a Marriage Partner
Copyright © 2012 by Jayce Tohline
http://tohline.com/

ISBN: 1479183385
ISBN-13: 978-1479183388

All rights reserved under International Copyright Law. Contents and/or cover may not be reproduced in whole or in part without the express written consent of the Publisher.

Introduction

About This Book

This book is written to help you find God's counsel concerning the person you plan to marry; finding out if that person is right for you.

My intent is to demonstrate the practical application of spiritual principles by using examples of how I found the will of God for marriage in my own life. This book is meant to help you understand and apply these principles so you can successfully obtain the Counsel of God for your own life.

What This Book is NOT

This is NOT a book on dating. The reader should use the principles in this book prior to marriage, to make sure they are uniting with the right person. The information in this book can even be valuable in the early stages of a dating relationship... at a point when the reader is wondering if the relationship should continue.

This is NOT a book about sexual morals. Though I could tell you why you should conduct your relationships in a chaste manner, your prior actions should not be used as an excuse why you can't get direction from God when choosing a marriage partner.

This is NOT a book about solving marriage problems. This book is intended for use prior to making the decision to marry someone. However, this book can help the reader learn how to "hear" God when faced with the difficult issues of life.

This is NOT a religious book. The basis of true Christianity is relationship, not religion (e.g. "law", "rules" and "regulations"). This book comes from a perspective of relationship with God... one where the reader can actually approach the Creator of the Universe and obtain answers from Him regarding the future.

Contents

How to Obtain the Counsel of the Lord 1

Positioning Yourself to Hear God 13

My Greatest Mistake 23

How I Avoided the Wrong Marriage Partner 27

How God Showed Me the Right Person to Marry 35

Recognizing Fear 43

A New Dimension of Prayer 51

Thoughts about Marriage 57

References 61

Book Store Orders 61

More Articles 53

Contact Information 53

Speaking Engagements 53

How to Obtain the Counsel of the Lord

Let's get this settled right away... You Can Hear God!

One of the most important "skills" any Christian can (and should) learn is the ability to purposely obtain specific direction from God when making crucial decisions. And there are few decisions more important to one's long-term well-being and happiness than that of choosing the "right" marriage partner.

God Wants to Speak to You

God wants your permission to speak to you... to help you... to provide direction... to become personally involved in your decisions... to be an integral part of your life. I grew up in a Christian denomination, yet the idea that God would "speak" to me was a foreign concept. As a young adult I came into contact with Christians who claimed that God actually did "speak" to them and give them direction in life. Though this was welcome news, it took me several years to understand HOW to purposely and effectively obtain the counsel of the Lord in a practical and consistent manner.

I hope this book will help you trim years off of the process in your own life.

God's Word is His Will

God reveals His general will through the Bible. What do I mean by this? Simply that the Bible reveals what God wants for everyone.

In the Bible He reveals the blessings He wants *everyone* to enjoy. He also reveals the principles through which *anyone* can obtain any of those blessings. That's what I mean by the "general" will of God.

You see, the Bible provides the *logos* of God. (In the original manuscripts for the New Testament, the Greek word "logos" refers to a "general" statement that applies to a group of people.) The *logos* of God (meaning the "Word" of God) provides the general will of God... you might say it provides "guidelines" for living. In the Gospel of John, Jesus is referred to as the Word of God (*logos of God*), demonstrating the will of God for healing, prayer, social interactions, and salvation for ALL mankind.

The Specific Will of God

But there are plenty of situations in life when you need more than just His general will... Specific answers to specific questions about YOUR life. Questions like, "Should I marry this woman I'm dating?" or "Should I purchase this car?" or "What school should I attend?" or "Should I go into business with this person?" or "Should I accept THIS job offer or THAT job offer?" There are plenty of decisions in life where we want to make right choices, and it would be good to receive guidance from the One who sees all and knows all.

The common thread through those questions is that the choice you make can have a future impact. Your choice can lead to happiness or pain, or contribute to your prosperity or bring lack, or stress, or sickness, or... (fill in the blank with your negative outcome). This is particularly true in decisions that will affect you for many years to come, or in those involving a significant amount of money.

In these types of decisions there is an inherent desire to "see" into the future. This is why many go to psychics for advice, or to astrologers. They want to see into the future, but end up depending on mere mortals without knowing the spiritual source of their advisor. Most people, even Christians, have no understanding that they can actually approach the Creator of the Universe, the God who "sees the end from the beginning"… the One who is willing to give them the direction they need so they can experience blessings in life, instead of leading a "cursed" existence.

> …I have set before you life and death, blessing and cursing; therefore choose life, that both you and your descendants may live.
>
> – Deuteronomy 30:19

> For I know the thoughts that I think toward you, says the LORD, thoughts of peace and not of evil, to give you a future and a hope.
>
> – Jeremiah 29:11

When considering marriage you want to know if the person you're considering will be a good choice for the long haul… for the many years of life you will experience together. You nor I can see the future, but we know the One who can. In fact, the Bible is the only holy book showing a "god" who can accurately tell us what will happen in the future. He has done it over and over throughout the scriptures, and His ability to see the future has not diminished.

Advice that will Stand the Test of Time

Take a look at this scripture…

> *There are many devices in a man's heart; nevertheless the counsel of the Lord, THAT shall stand.*
> *– Proverbs 19:21 (KJV)*

When seeking counsel, you want to obtain something that will STAND... something that will stand the test of time... something that will prove out as correct. This verse promises that the counsel of the Lord will be the advice that will STAND.

The main obstacle you will often encounter in determining God's specific direction in life involves the "devices" that are established in your heart.

The Hebrew word translated here as "devices" is also translated as "thoughts", "plans" and "inventions".

When you look to God for counsel you have to sift through your *own* thoughts and plans (particularly those you have become emotionally tied to) and be willing to discard *your* thoughts for *His* thoughts. You see, much of our thinking is flawed to begin with... many of our personal convictions may actually be our own inventions... or the inventions of those we've chosen to listen to. These thoughts simply don't line up with God's truth, though they may seem logical and acceptable to *you*.

In the New Testament, Paul says we should not be "ignorant of (Satan's) devices" (2 Corinthians 2:11 KJV). The Greek word translated here as "devices" can be translated as "mind games".

Now, when you realize Satan is "the god of this world (system)" (2 Corinthians 4:4 KJV), and his tactic is to "blind the minds" of people – keeping them away from TRUTH... keeping them in unbelief... keeping them AWAY from the *true* counsel of God –

we begin to see that Satan will use physical evidence to keep us from perceiving spiritual truth.

In essence, your main challenge is to move beyond what your mind perceives and understands. The mind is limited to the evidence it can gain through our five senses. If we can get in touch with God, we will be able to "see" beyond the "natural" and learn the spiritual truth of a matter. And that spiritual perspective can also include an understanding based on future events.

He Never Lost a Dime in His Investments

I was once told of a man who began investing at a young age. Each investment he made was solid, and over time his wealth grew. Word got around that he was a wealthy man, and those wanting to start new businesses would approach him for funding. He said some of those opportunities, based on the evidence he had, looked like they were sure winners. Others seemed a waste of his time. In either case, he followed the same process to find *God's* opinion.

The success of his method was startling, as he claimed he "never lost a dime" in any of his investments.

Here's how he did it...

His Process for Seeking God

He would first take the information about the investment opportunity and make sure he understood it.

He would then separate himself from all outside influence and interruptions. For this purpose he had a closet that was large enough to hold a chair where he could close the door and sit comfortably.

He told his wife not to bother him... "If I get hungry, I'll come out and eat... but don't bother calling me for meals, and just take messages if anyone calls."

He would usually begin these sessions by reading his Bible. [I like to start in Proverbs.]

He would also pray, asking God to reveal the right decision.

But most of the time he would sit quietly before the Lord.

He would pursue this process until he had his answer. By his account, the process sometimes took as little as an hour, but never more than 3 days. In each case, the decision he got from the Lord proved profitable.

Interestingly, when God said "no" to an investment, this man made it a practice to follow the progress of that business. Each of the businesses in which God told him NOT to invest ended up losing money or failing. Now realize, *his initial impression* for a number of those opportunities had been, "This can't possibly fail."

On the flip side, some of the opportunities he initially thought could *not* make it were ones where God had given him "the green light"... and each of those became profitable investments for him.

How would you like to own a successful investing record like that?

Key Points You Should Know

Here are some things you need to be aware of as you learn to seek God.

1) Don't be moved by outward appearance or physical evidence.

Many choices appear to be no-brainers. If it's a big choice that involves large sums of money, or the investment of years (e.g. marriage), seek to obtain the counsel of God.

In the book of Joshua we find a great example of the dangers of decisions based on physical evidence and assumption.

After the huge victory at Jericho, Joshua sent a small contingent of his men to capture the little town of Ai (Joshua, chapter 7). To Joshua and his men this was a no-brainer. Based on their reconnaissance it was determined this would be an easy battle to win.

Joshua then sent a contingent of only 3,000 warriors, and they were soundly defeated. Why? They had made their decision based on physical evidence (what they could determine with their five senses) and had neglected to seek the counsel of God.

2) Simplify the question you submit to God

It's only natural to want God to tell us the entire story. I don't know about you, but I'm just not spiritual enough to "hear" that much detail. I need something easier to understand.

If at all possible, I boil my question down so the answer can be a "yes" or a "no". This is a Biblical approach, too…

In the Old Testament the leaders of Israel were to seek the counsel of God through the High Priest. Part of the High Priest's garment (uniform) included a breastplate containing the Urim and Thummim[1]. Jewish tradition holds that one of these two jewels would glow in response to a question posed to God... one of the jewels represented "yes", and the other represented "no".

So... all Joshua would have had to do was to go to the High Priest and ask, "Should we go up against Ai?" An answer of "no" could have led to more questions... and through a process of seeking God (kind of like playing "20 questions") they would have found out what to do, and the lives of his warriors could have been saved.

3) Include Fasting in your plan

In 2 Chronicles, chapter 20, three enemy armies joined forces to attack Israel. The enemy had overwhelming numbers. Israel's king, Jehoshaphat, knew he needed direction from the Lord, and he needed it quickly. So he called his people together to fast (give up eating food) until they received an answer from God. In the end, the answer came and God defeated the enemy before the army of Israel could even get to the battle field.

I've heard people talk about fasting like it's a magic wand. It's not... there's nothing magical or mystical about it. And fasting won't "twist God's arm" and force Him to answer more quickly (or force Him to do something that's against His will). Choosing to fast is like saying, "I want the answer so much that I would rather spend the time seeking God than eating. The desire for food has become secondary to my desire for the counsel of God."

And the Bible says "you will find Him IF you seek Him with all your heart and with all your soul." (Deuteronomy 4:29)

The more seriously you want to hear from Him, the more likely you will hear.

4) Believe God will reward you with the answer you need.

> "... anyone who comes to him must believe that he exists and that he rewards those who **earnestly** seek him."
>
> – *Hebrews 11:6 (NIV)*

(The bold type is added by the author for emphasis.)

5) Be determined to get the answer

If obtaining the counsel of God is really important to you, then make the decision you're going to continue to pursue the answer until you get it. Anything short of that is an indication that finding God's counsel wasn't really important to you after all.

In the earlier example we see the investor sometimes had to spend as many as 3 days of separated time. You may have a situation keeping you from taking that much time away from all your responsibilities... like a job.

There have been times I had to make an important decision, but I had to work, too. In those situations I have grabbed whatever time I could and devoted it to prayer... I have prayed while walking from my desk to the copier, or to the restroom. I have taken lunch breaks by myself so I could spend time alone with God. I have even gotten up in the middle of the night with a desire to pray.

Utilize driving time and turn your car into a prayer chamber. Exchange television (or internet) time for prayer time. Drop every unnecessary chore or distraction so you can turn your mind and heart to God. What you "give up" indicates your true priority, and reveals your determination.

Grabbing small segments of time will likely cause the overall process to take longer than 3 days. In my experience, though, when I have stuck with the process I have always received God's answer.

Jesus said it this way:

> *"Keep on asking and it will be given you; keep on seeking and you will find; keep on knocking [reverently] and [the door] will be opened to you. For everyone who keeps on asking receives; and he who keeps on seeking finds; and to him who keeps on knocking, [the door] will be opened."*
> *– Matthew 7:7 (AMP)*

How the Answer Comes

People ask me, "But how will I know when I've heard His voice? How will I know when I have the answer?"

My answer to that is, "You will know."

I can't really describe it to you, but the first time you go all the way through the process, you will understand what I'm talking about.

You see, we talk about "hearing" God... but that's really a worldly (physical) attempt to describe what happens when God speaks to us.

God speaks to the heart, not to our ears.

His "voice" is the voice of PEACE.

THAT is what you're looking for... a "peace that passes all understanding²", and the result of that peace is Faith... a "knowing" on the inside that you have the right answer... no matter what the world's evidence might be.

> *"And let the peace from Christ rule (act as an **umpire** continually) in your hearts [deciding and settling with finality all questions that arise in your minds]..."*
> – *Colossians 3:15 (AMP)*

✦ Things to Consider ✦

- You can "hear" God. It just requires some effort you your part.

- The enemy wants to set you up for failure. Through "mind games" he will try to persuade you to be satisfied with evidence gathered by your physical senses. But your physical senses cannot determine the future. Only God can do that.

- The less emotion you have concerning the situation, the easier it will be to "hear" God. Emotions cloud one's ability to find God's counsel because we become less willing to part with whatever the emotions have tied us to. (This is just as important in other matters, like purchasing a car or house. The fewer emotions you have that tie you to a specific choice, the easier it will be to find God's peace.) You must be willing to walk away from the situation if God says, "No."

- God's "voice" is compared to PEACE. Colossians 3:15 (above) compares that peace to an umpire. In the game of baseball the umpire's decision is final. A player may not like the umpire's decision and begin to argue. He may get right in the umpire's face and yell and wave his arms in anger and intimidation; but the umpire's mind will not change. His call stands. That's how strong the peace of God can be... Once you receive it in your heart, the world around you can seem like it's falling apart, but the peace of God will continue to stand.

- Seek God with all your heart, for those who seek Him with all their heart will find the answer they need.

"... you will seek the LORD your God, and you will find [Him] if you seek Him with all your heart and with all your soul."
– Deuteronomy 4:29

Positioning Yourself to Hear God

*There are, it may be, so many
kinds of voices in the world,
and none of them [is] without
signification.*
~ 1 Corinthians 14:10 (KJV) ~

The Phone Call

Have you ever received a phone call from someone who just assumed you knew who they were? After you said, "Hello", they began talking about something without giving their name, and you were thinking, "Who is this?"

You probably didn't know who they were because you hadn't spent a lot of time talking to them on the phone. You hadn't HEARD their voice often enough to identify it when they called.

But there are some who don't need to identify themselves. When they call and begin to speak you know exactly who they are. Why? Because you've spent time hearing them speak. You know the sound of their voice, the manner in which they talk, and the types of things they say.

Hearing God is a lot like that. If you've been listening to Him talk it will be a lot easier to recognize Him when He provides counsel and direction.

Learning God's Voice

Reading the scriptures is like familiarizing yourself with the way God speaks. (I don't mean "King James English". I mean the kinds of things He will say... the concepts and the character behind His ways of thinking.) The more familiar you become with His "Word", the easier it will be to distinguish His "voice".

God shows us His will through the scriptures. I like to say it this way: "The Bible is God speaking to me."

> *For [as] the heavens are higher than the earth, so are My ways higher than your ways, and My thoughts than your thoughts. For as the rain comes down, and the snow from heaven, and do not return there, but water the earth, and make it bring forth and bud, that it may give seed to the sower and bread to the eater, so shall My word be that goes forth from My mouth; It shall not return to Me void, but it shall accomplish what I please, and it shall prosper [in the thing] for which I sent it.*
> *– Isaiah 55:9-11*

God knows we don't think like Him. We've been surrounded by the world system all our lives, and the world system runs counter to the way God does things. Because He is aware of this, He has provided His thoughts in a form that allows us to see and hear the very things that will enable us to make right choices.

> *This Book of the Law [the Bible] shall not depart from your mouth, but you shall meditate in it day and night, that you may observe to do according to all that is written in it. For* **then** *you will make your way prosperous, and then you will have good success.*
> *– Joshua 1:8 (Bold added for emphasis)*

When we choose to meditate on the things we find in the scriptures, particularly those things found in Proverbs and the letters Paul wrote to the churches in the New Testament, we will find God's keys to an abundant and prosperous life... keys to relationships, financial decisions, health, and so on.

Armed with your understanding of the way God "thinks", you'll be better equipped to see the heart of the person you're in relationship with. You'll be able to compare what they do and say to what God says is "right".

Uncovering the "Real" Person

Many mistakes are made in relationships (and in business) by judging situations based on physical evidence. It was said of Jesus, though, that He knew what was in the hearts of men... His assessment went beyond the surface presentation to the very core of the people He dealt with.

Like God, Jesus looked at the heart of a person and wasn't moved (influenced) by their outward appearance.

In Matthew, Jesus provides a key to seeing what's really in a person's heart... seeing who they "really" are at their core. How? Simply listen to them.

That's right... Listen to them talk.

> *"...For out of the abundance of the heart the mouth speaks."*
> *– Matthew 12:34*

Listen to their words, and the attitude behind what they say.

Are they merciful or judgmental?

Are they condescending, or do they point to the good in others?

Do they blame everyone else for their problems, or do they take responsibility for their decisions and their situation?

Is their attitude and outlook negative or positive?

Do they lie, or do they tell the truth?

How do they treat others who could in no way be a benefit to them? (That's likely how they will treat you when you can no longer benefit them.)

> *A good man out of the good treasure of his heart brings forth good things, and an evil man out of the evil treasure brings forth evil things.*
> *– Matthew 12:35*

Notice Jesus compares the heart (the core of a person) to a treasure chest (or a bank account). Why? Because you can't take something out of a bank that you didn't deposit into it.

How can one take jewels out of a treasure chest when all they've put into it is pig slop?

> *How can you, being evil, speak good things? For out of the abundance of the heart the mouth speaks.*
> *– Matthew 12:34*

In the same way, one cannot draw words and actions out of their heart that differ from the deposits they have made into their heart.

How a person talks will reveal their deposits... their thought life... because "out of the abundance of the heart the mouth speaks."

Words (and actions) reveal a lot about who a person *really* is. They may be "nice" to you, but how do they treat others? How do they treat their parents, their siblings, their co-workers, or those who are less fortunate? Anyone can be nice when they want to impress someone... but they can't keep up the act in all situations, and a thin veneer will wear away in abrasive situations.

Words reveal character... they reveal the "real" person on the inside... the one behind the mask... the one behind the façade. Like in the movie *The Wizard of Oz*, the "man behind the curtain" is revealed by the words coming out of his mouth.

Spotting the Counterfeit

Jesus is compared to a shepherd whose sheep follow him because they know his voice. The same sheep will run away from a stranger because they aren't familiar with *his* voice.

> *And when he brings out his own sheep, he goes before them; and the sheep follow him, for they know his voice. Yet they will by no means follow a stranger, but will flee from him, for they do not know the voice of strangers.*
> – John 10:4-5

Notice that the "stranger" is recognized because the sheep are familiar with a specific voice.

I've been told that individuals in the FBI and the Banking Industry learn how to recognize counterfeit currency by becoming intimately familiar with real currency. They handle the real money, they examine its detail, and they learn how it feels to the touch. Then, when they are presented with a counterfeit bill they can recognize it because it just doesn't feel right, and the details are not right. It is "different" than what they are used to.

Again... How can you KNOW when God is the one speaking to you if you haven't spent enough time with God to know the way He talks?

The Con Artist

God is a spirit, but God is not the only spirit attempting to gain your attention.

> *There are, it may be, so many kinds of voices in the world, and none of them [is] without signification.*
> *– 1 Corinthians 14:10 (KJV)*

This is why you should become familiar with God through reading and meditating on scriptures from the Bible. If you learn how God speaks... what He "sounds" like... the kinds of things He "says"... His attitude toward you and toward others... If you learn how God speaks, you'll be better equipped to identify when the voice you hear is NOT God.

Any con man can call you on the phone, provide a false name and an "official" title, and try to convince you to do something that will put you (or your family, or your finances) at risk.

If the "voice" you "hear" claims to be "God", but doesn't sound like God, then don't do what the "voice" tells you to do!

> *The thief does not come except to steal, and to kill, and to destroy. I have come that they may have life, and that they may have [it] more abundantly.*

> *I am the good shepherd. The good shepherd gives His life for the sheep.*
>
> *– Jesus, in John 10:10-11*

You have an unseen enemy who wants to mislead you... to send you down the wrong path... a path of unhappiness, unfulfillment, and even destruction.

This advice also applies to counsel you receive from others... even from those you "trust".

In the important decisions of life, do your due diligence and press through until you receive God's counsel. There are many lives who have been horribly affected because they chose their marriage partner based on the counsel of a psychic... or even a Christian minister.

(I remember counseling one couple who were thoroughly unhappy in their marriage. It turns out that they had married because their "minister" had told them it was God's will that they marry.)

YOU can learn to hear God's voice. YOU can learn to get God's counsel. Through Jesus Christ, YOU have been given direct access to God, Himself. You don't have to go through other people to get to God. You don't have to rely on someone else's "spiritual sensitivity". Why put your future at risk when you can know YOU have made the "right" decision.

I Heard the Wrong Voice

I remember one time, early in my Christian walk, a day when I had really blown it. I knew I had sinned.

But, because I had been listening to an audio series about 1 John 1:9, I realized I could confess my sin to God and receive immediate forgiveness.

> *If we confess our sins, He is faithful and just to forgive us [our] sins and to cleanse us from all unrighteousness.*
> *– 1 John 1:9*

Well, it didn't take me long to admit to God that I had sinned and to ask for His forgiveness. I then thanked Him for restoring me to right-standing with Him.

Later that evening I was in my room and the memory of what I had done came back to me. I mulled it over for a few moments, feeling badly about what I had done, when a "voice" came to me saying, "Boy, you really messed up today, didn't you?"

I immediately responded, "Yes, Lord, I really blew it." And I began to feel even more dejected and sorry for myself. Feelings of religious condemnation swept through me as I considered what I had done.

Then it occurred to me... "Wait! That couldn't be the *Lord* talking to me, because the Bible says when He forgives my sin He WILL NOT remember it!

> *I, [even] I, [am] He who blots out your transgressions for My own sake; And I will not remember your sins.*
> *– Isaiah 43:25*

If *anyone* was remembering my sin it was the devil, not my God. I had already received forgiveness from God, and I knew He is faithful to His promise.

Because I had information about what God would say in that situation, I caught the enemy red-handed. He was trying to pass himself off as the Lord so he could work condemnation and false leading in my life. He was trying to make me feel guilty, sinful and unworthy, to drive a wedge between me and God.

Because I had planted scriptures in my heart I was able to recognize the "voice" that came to me. By that one scripture I was able to defeat the enemy's plan, and I rejoiced in the faithfulness of my Father.

> *"For the word of God [is]... a discerner of the THOUGHTS and intents of the heart."*
>
> *– Hebrews 4:12*

Knowing scripture can help you recognize a counterfeit who poses as "the voice of the Lord" to lead you astray.

✦ Things to Consider ✦

- Spending time reading and meditating scripture enhances your ability to "hear" God.

- Character is of primary importance when looking for someone with whom you will spend the rest of your life.

- Objectivity in "listening" to the words and attitudes coming out of the mouth of others will help you learn a lot about who they "really" are.

- Familiarity with scripture puts you in position to recognize when thoughts or words of counsel are NOT from God.

- You don't need to seek guidance from psychics or from others when you know how to get your counsel directly from God.

"...Listen to me, [my] children, for blessed [are those who] keep my ways. Hear instruction and be wise, and do not disdain [it]. Blessed is the man who listens to me, watching daily at my gates, waiting at the posts of my doors. For whoever finds me finds life, and obtains favor from the LORD; but he who sins against me wrongs his own soul; all those who hate me love death."
– Proverbs 8:32-36

My Greatest Mistake

For as many as are led by the Spirit of God, these are sons of God.

~ Romans 8:14 ~

The subject of this mini-book is so dear to me because I experienced the heartbreak of being in a "wrong" marriage.

Internal Warning Signals

I was 25 years old and engaged to a young woman I met in college. We had been together for about 3 years and planned to spend the rest of our lives together.

The closer we approached the wedding date, the more I felt uneasy about going through with the ceremony. Deep inside it felt like I was making a mistake. It was a "gut feeling", if you will.

How did it feel? It felt "scratchy" on the inside. It was a foreboding feeling. "Something" just wasn't right about the situation.

At one point, about a month before the wedding, I tried to break it off. In the face of her tears, though, I caved in and said I would go through with the ceremony.

As I walked into the church for our wedding I knew I was making a mistake. I just didn't have the courage to say, "No. This isn't right, and I'm not going through with it."

I didn't want to hurt anyone's feelings, but in the end, I inflicted more pain than if I had just obeyed the "inward witness" – my "gut feeling".

Three years later we broke it off and went our separate ways.

Does God Speak to Non-Christians?

I was raised in a church-going family, but at age 25 I could not truthfully call myself a Christian. Looking back, though, I see God was trying to convince me to change my decision about that marriage. I didn't understand that the foreboding feeling down in my core was His "voice", but it was there... in a very strong way.

God loves us all. Because of His great, unselfish love, He always tries to nudge us onto the right path. He's doing His best with what He has to work with, but ultimately it's our choice to listen to Him or to turn a deaf ear. I chose to override the urging I had inside... partly from ignorance, but mostly because I reasoned it away. Why? I didn't have the COURAGE to break off the relationship before we reached the altar.

Here's my point:

I wasn't a Christian, yet God was still trying to get my attention so He could keep me from making a huge mistake!

How much MORE does He want to help those who have given their life to Him through Jesus Christ?

✦ **Things to Consider** ✦

- Learn to be honest with yourself. Are you feeling a "red light" on the inside of you? Are you overlooking warning signs because you "want" things to work out the way you had planned?

- Be careful of your emotions for another person. When you become emotionally involved you will be less likely to let go of that relationship when it's time to let go.

- PAY ATTENTION to your "gut" feeling.

- Don't be a "wimp". Have the **courage** to do what's "right".

How I Avoided the Wrong Marriage Partner

"Keep on asking and it will be given you; keep on seeking and you will find; keep on knocking and [the door] will be opened to you."
~ Matthew 7:7 (Amplified) ~

I look back on my life in Christ and am thankful for His leading. I am amazed at how He led me when I was a young Christian… how He was able to break through into my consciousness even when I didn't know much. I believe my success in following His leading was because I devoted much of my time in those early days to teaching tapes and books about Faith and Prayer. That time helped increase my sensitivity to His "voice".

Beginning the Relationship

I received Salvation shortly after the events of the previous chapter. Soon after the divorce I was introduced to a young woman, and we began to date. The life she and her family lived in front of me convinced me there was a God, and that a relationship with Him was exactly what I wanted in my life. As a result, I asked her to lead me in a prayer for salvation, where I accepted Jesus as my Lord and Savior.

After I became a Christian the relationship with this young woman grew. It seemed we fit together in so many ways. As I grew in the Lord, my love for her also grew. Within a few months I asked her to marry me, and she accepted.

Over the next couple of years I tried to get her to set a date for marriage, but she resisted. She had been married previously, as had I, and I think she was nervous about taking that step again.

During our courtship I obtained a contract to do some work for an oil company in another state. This meant the two of us had to carry on a long distance relationship, seeing each other once every month or two. Still, the relationship grew, and I was quite happy with the situation.

I became Aware

We were finally getting close to setting a date when an event took place in my life that made me aware I had never asked the Lord about His will concerning my choice for a marriage partner. I had come into my Christian walk emotionally attached to this woman, and realized that I had just assumed our marriage was a good thing. She was a Christian, and she had led me to Christ. She was intelligent, I was intelligent. We enjoyed a lot of the same things, and had hopes and dreams concerning our future together.

This new awareness, though, hit me like a brick. Of all the things I was concerned about, who I decided to spend the rest of my life with should have been the most important. I had already gone through one wrong marriage. I didn't want to make the same mistake again. And who would know about the future better than God, who knows all and sees all?

It was disconcerting to me that it had never dawned on me to ask HIS advice and counsel in the matter. While I really had no concept of how I would find out, I was determined I WOULD find His will and make my decision based on that knowledge.

Immediately I decided I needed to spend time in prayer. I had a job to perform, so I couldn't just drop everything and shut myself in a closet. What I could do, though, was pray at every opportunity.

During the Days

Over the next few days my job assignments required a lot of driving. I spent hours each day praying in my car. At every available moment during the day my mind would turn to the issue at hand, and I would turn my heart to God in prayer. There was a burning desire to know His will about this situation.

There were times when, as I was driving, I would break out in tremendous sobbing and tears. It was a heart-wrenching time for me. I was laying it all on the line and saying, "God, whatever you want for me... whatever you think is best... THAT is what I will do... no matter how much it may hurt. Why? Because YOU know best."

In the Evenings

At night I would arrive back at my house, prepare my evening meal, then sit down with my Bible. I wanted to focus my mind on the things of God... and I wanted WISDOM. I started each evening by reading passages in the book of Proverbs. I would then talk to God and pour out my heart... I would pray... and I would read my Bible... until it was time for bed.

The next day I would do it all over again.

How Long Does It Take?

It really didn't matter to me how much time it would take to hear God. I wanted to KNOW more than anything else in the world. I wanted to know, more than I wanted food, more than I wanted sleep, more than I wanted social interaction with others. I was willing to take as long as necessary to get the answer.

There were times when I would think, "My God... this is hard. How much longer will I need to do this?" This was just my "flesh" wanting something valuable with little investment. Going through this process was "work", and the "lazy" part of me wanted to say it was too hard, and convince me to just give up and go ahead with my original plan.

Suddenly

Then, late one morning, on the 10th day of prayer, I drove out of town to work in a neighboring county. As I was praying, PEACE dropped into my heart... into the core of my being. All of a sudden I KNEW the answer... there was no doubt in my heart or mind about it. It was so monumental to me that I can take you back to the place in the road where it happened. I "knew that I knew that I knew that I knew". And I knew that the only one who could talk me out of that "knowing" would be me.

The answer? I think you've guessed by now... The answer was, "No. Don't marry her."

Sad? Yes. But I knew it was right. The PEACE was there.

Why did God tell me NO? I don't know for sure. I have some theories. But it really didn't matter at the time. I didn't need to know the why... I just needed to know that my Heavenly Father loves me, and he knows what is best for me. So why argue? Why turn away from His counsel? Why do it my way when I knew I'd be setting myself up for failure by going against His counsel?

The peace I had was so strong... so real. It settled the question... finally... once and for all.

Peace – The Umpire

> "And let the peace (soul harmony which comes) from Christ rule (act as an **umpire** continually) in your hearts [deciding and settling with finality all questions that arise in your minds]..."
> – Colossians 3:15 (Amplified)

In baseball the umpire is "king". Whatever he says is the final decision. The batter can yell, the manager can yell, they can wave their arms angrily and go through all kinds of theatricals... but whatever the Umpire has said is the final decision.

In the above verse we see the correlation. When you receive PEACE FROM GOD, let that peace rule... let it settle WITH ALL FINALITY any question that may arise.

Some of my friends couldn't understand the decision I had made. Some even suggested that I hadn't heard God... that I hadn't received enough counsel from others. But I had the "word of the Lord" on it... I had "prayed through" and had obtained His peace... His knowing. That peace made it easy to stand in the face of their questions, even though I didn't know all the answers. I still knew what THE answer was, and that was the one I was sticking with.

Was it easy walking it out? Was it easy breaking the news to her, and to her family? No... but it was right.

How Will I Know?

People have asked me, "How will I know when I get the answer?"

The only thing I can say is, "You will know."

If you stick with it... if you are determined... you will know. And then you will know how to get an answer from God on practically anything else. All you'll have to do is decide it's worth the time and the effort to continue seeking Him until the answer is revealed."

This may be the most important kind of prayer you will ever learn...

> "Keep on asking and it will be given you; keep on seeking and you will find; keep on knocking and [the door] will be opened to you."
> – Jesus (Matthew 7:7 – Amplified)
>
> "... (God) is a rewarder of them that diligently seek him."
> – Hebrews 11:6

✦ Things to Consider ✦

- Remember... God loves you, and only wants the best for you. You must be willing to give yourself over to His answer, no matter how emotionally hard it might be.

- If getting the right answer is important enough to you, you will take the amount of time that's necessary to get the answer.

- You are seeking counsel based on "hidden" things that can't be seen. God can not only see the future, He can see what's in YOUR heart and in the heart of the person you're considering as a marriage partner.

- You may be tempted to get the answer from another person, but they can't see what God sees. They don't know what God knows. Learn to go to God for yourself and you'll know to get the "right" answer.

- Peace from God provides courage in the face of opposition.

"Therefore judge nothing before the time, until the Lord comes, who will both bring to light the hidden things of darkness and reveal the counsels of the hearts. Then each one's praise will come from God."

– 1 Corinthians 4:5

How God Showed Me the Right Person to Marry

One moment you're sitting there, minding your own business. The next moment you're suddenly aware God has visited you, the sky has opened up, and your life is now very different.

Early in my Christian walk I learned that God has a purpose for each life. After the events of the previous chapter, I also became aware that I was looking for someone who would compliment what I was "called" to do... someone who would be a PARTNER in LIFE.

The Qualities I was Looking For

I made a list... not one that was written on paper, but one that was very much alive in my heart and head. The Lord had directed me to break off a relationship in which the woman possessed a lot of attributes that appealed to me. I was not about to settle for less than what God had told me to leave, so I had a list of things I was *unwilling to live WITHOUT*.

I had also experienced a failed marriage, so there was another list... a list of the things I was *unwilling to live WITH*.

I certainly didn't abstain from dating... and there were a few women who were appealing enough to prayerfully consider. But as each of those relationships fell by the wayside I would say to God, "You're just making it harder on yourself to bring me the right marriage partner. I've now added to the list of qualities I'm unwilling to live without, and I've added to the list of traits I'm unwilling to live with. So it's going to be pretty difficult for You to bring me someone who matches my lists."

We Met

Diane and I met Friday night, February 13, 1981. We were introduced by a common friend who thought it was her business to be a match-maker for me. I ended up joining Diane and some friends at a pizza parlor, and then I gave her a ride home. Soon we were dating, and spending a LOT of time together.

As the relationship progressed, the difficult thing for me was to keep the emotions at bay. I had learned this was a necessary element in being able to hear God, so I worked hard at keeping a level head... because I wanted to KNOW. I wanted to "hear" God. I didn't want to be tricked by emotions into a relationship that wouldn't work.

I wanted someone who would go the distance... who would stick by my side through thick and thin... someone who would be my partner in anything WE attempted. I didn't want emotions fogging my mind and messing with my ability to hear God.

It's hard to walk away from something that isn't right when you're emotionally attached to it.

I Heard

Now get the picture... I wanted to hear God... I wanted His direction in this relationship. That was first and foremost in my thought life.

Of course I was looking for a wife. I WANTED to get married. But I wanted God's stamp of approval MUCH more than I wanted marriage. While some people are in love with being in love, my love for God was first and foremost. I wanted God's love for me to pave the way to something that would be successful.

About three weeks into our relationship Diane and I went to a park and sat on a bench to talk. I remember the event clearly. It was just after noon, and it was a beautiful day. As we visited I experienced that sensation of PEACE. It dropped into me in the same way it had dropped into me in the previous chapter… only this time the answer was clearly YES.

It's difficult to explain it to someone else. One moment you're sitting there, minding your own business. The next moment you're suddenly aware God has visited you, the sky has opened up, and your life is now very different. I KNEW this relationship was right. And immediately following this flood of peace were emotions for Diane that began to rise up and take over.

I didn't dare say anything. This was such an unexpected event that I wanted to "sit" on it for a while… to be sure I was hearing God and that I wasn't being influenced by emotions. I knew if I began to talk at that moment that the experience would bubble over and I would get lost in the emotions that were now overwhelming me.

I simply said, "Diane, I need to go. Let me take you back to your apartment. I'll talk to you later."

She may have asked what I needed to do… If she did, I'm sure I said something like, "I just need to be alone for a little while."

She was kind enough to go with the flow, and I took her back home. I then drove to a quiet place and sat quietly for a while. I soon became settled that I had heard God... I then went to a florist, bought a dozen salmon-colored roses, and took them to Diane. I then turned around and left again because I didn't want to open my mouth and let a flood of words out... it just wasn't time, yet.

The Proposal

About a week later Diane and I drove to the mountains to spend the day sightseeing. On the way I determined it was time to ask her to marry me. I didn't really have a plan. (What I did then would never work for today's young people. They have to have some EVENT for the proposal, and everyone is trying to outdo other proposals.) As we ate lunch together I asked her... and, surprised as she was, she said, "Yes."

We finished our day of sightseeing and, on the way back home, we began to talk about the wedding and the honeymoon... making fun plans... relishing the moment. When we got back to town she even had me go into a drug store to buy some Bride magazines (so no one would see HER buying them).

The Retraction

The next day she came to me, saying she was feeling uneasy about saying yes, and that she really wasn't sure about the whole thing.

While that news was surprising, it didn't shake the peace on the inside of me. I wanted HER to have the same assurance I had. I simply said, "That's okay. You need to do what you need to do. I know what I know. You need to know, too."

A few days later (I think it was only three or four days) she came back to me and said, "I know, now. I'm ready, and the answer is yes."

If she had said, "No."

Looking back, if she had come back with a "no", I would have let it go. Please realize... God doesn't have just one person who can be a good match for you. God is not that small. He has others who can match up with you and be what you need. One person's "no" cannot upset God's plan and purpose for your life.

Would it have been disappointing? Yes. But the peace inside of me was bigger than anything that could have happened. That peace also said, "Everything will work out. Don't worry about it."

Marriage

At the time of this writing, Diane and I will soon celebrate our 31st anniversary. Each of us will tell you it hasn't been the easiest journey. There have been a lot of potholes... some almost big enough to swallow us up. But we agreed that "divorce" would not be a part of our vocabulary. Were there times when we were tempted to say that word? Yes... several. But we had BOTH heard God. We had that anchor... that point in time in each of our lives we could go back to and say, "NO! I heard God, and this marriage is right. He wouldn't lie, so I'm not giving up!"

This is important: BOTH need to know. Both need to have that place... that landmark to go back to... to be able to remember and recommit to the peace that marked that spot in the journey. If you don't have that landmark, I don't know how you can stand through the hard times.

Today, Diane and I love each other more than ever. There are so many things we've accomplished together, and as we look into the coming years there are so many more things we want to do... together. Our lives run parallel. When one has a victory, we both have that victory. When one is lagging behind, the other is there to pull them forward.

Hearing God... such a wonderful thing to learn... because He is RIGHT... ALL the time.

> "Keep on asking and it will be given you; keep on seeking and you will find; keep on knocking and [the door] will be opened to you."
>
> – *Matthew 7:7 (Amplified)*

> "And let the peace (soul harmony which comes) from Christ rule (act as an **umpire** continually) in your hearts [deciding and settling with finality all questions that arise in your minds]..."
>
> – *Colossians 3:15 (Amplified)*

✦ Things to Consider ✦

- PEACE means that everything will work out right... even though it doesn't look like it. Trust God. If He said YES, then He has it all figured out... for YOUR good.

- A person's character is of primary importance. You may think you know the other person's character, but God is the one who sees to the very core of each person. He knows the ones who will be faithful, and those who won't. Let Him sort it out. All you need to know is that He said YES or NO.

- When you receive "the answer", sit on it for a few days. Allow yourself time to be sure you have "peace" and not "emotion".

- When you KNOW, act on what you know.

"And all these blessings shall come upon you and overtake you, because you obey the voice of the LORD your God..."
– Deuteronomy 28:2

Recognizing Fear

*Sometimes we attract what we
don't want (or need).*

Faith is the currency of Heaven. It is the medium of exchange used in life and in prayer. Basically, what you believe (in your heart) is what you will be rewarded with.

Peace and Assurance

A working definition of Faith is ASSURANCE. The New Testament writers also used other terms to indicate the existence of Faith, such as "Confidence" and "Full Persuasion".

Faith is an inward assurance… a "peace"… a "know that I know that I know" on the inside that stands up (if it has to) in the face of contrary (natural) evidence with a quiet confidence.

When we have Faith we have an inward witness that something not yet seen will surely come to pass. In fact, the thing you "know" can be so "real" that you feel like it already exists… it just can't be "seen" yet.

It is an *inward* confidence because it is of the heart, not of the head. It is not a logical process, but a knowing on the inside that logic cannot shake. As a result, one can then speak or act in the face of contrary circumstance, and not be concerned about failure.

If a child in the first grade would define Faith, he might say, "I'm sure." That's what Faith is… ASSURANCE… being SURE on the inside. In fact, if you go through the New Testament and substitute the word "assurance" when you see the word "faith", you will have a greater understanding of what faith really is.

How Fear Works

Fear is like faith. While faith is positive, fear operates in the negative. Faith looks toward things you want and desire... things that are beneficial. Fear looks toward things that will take from you... things that will harm or hurt.

> *The thief does not come except to steal, and to kill, and to destroy. I have come that they may have life, and that they may have it more abundantly.*
> *– Jesus (John 10:10)*

You've seen a vehicle moving in reverse, haven't you? If you took a picture of that car and showed it to someone else, though, they might say the car is going forward. After all, the nose of the car is aimed in the "right" direction. When the car is in reverse, though, it is actually traveling *away from* its *apparent* destination.

Why am I talking about this in the context of marriage?

Fear is much like the reverse gear in a vehicle. You might THINK you are pointed where you WANT to go, but if your motives are fear-based you're actually moving in the opposite direction... AWAY from what you want.

Someone Who Lost it All

You've probably heard the Bible story of Job. At the beginning of the story he was a very wealthy man who had everything anyone could want, including a wonderful family. We also find a man who is concerned about his children and their well-being. He was a religious man, and was worried his children might "sin against God". So he became proactive and offered sacrifices for all of them after every one of their family gatherings *in case* any of them had sinned against God in their hearts.

It LOOKED like he was going in the right direction. After all, his actions showed his devotion to God. But then "all hell broke loose". Not only were his children killed, but calamities took his possessions and his livelihood.

After all his losses Job made an astounding statement.

> *"For the thing I greatly feared has come upon me, and what I dreaded has happened to me."*
> *– Job 3:25*

To an outsider it would have looked like Job was always heading in the right direction. He was doing all the "right" things. He was following religious protocol. You and I would have said, "He is faultless."

In fact, Job's "vehicle" so looked like it was pointed in the right direction that it even fooled Satan. In the devil's eyes it appeared that Job was righteous... spiritually untouchable. So much so that he asked GOD to attack Job.

Listen to what God then said. "LOOK, he is in your power." (Job 2:6). Notice God didn't say, "I'm giving him over to you, Devil." Instead, He said, "LOOK... Job IS in your power." (BUT, Mr. Devil, since you couldn't see that, I'm going to put a limit on your actions and forbid you to kill him.)

Can you see it? Job's actions were so convincing that he fooled those around him, he fooled Satan, and he fooled himself. BUT

God, who sees the heart of man, saw clearly. The man was operating in FEAR, and his actions were sown in FEAR, and "what a man sows, THAT shall he reap.[3]"

Spiritual law does not fail.

Here's my point...

You need to be honest with your self-assessment when you're looking for a marriage partner. Take a hard look at WHY you want a marriage partner with certain qualities. If your motives are wrong, you may actually get the opposite of what you want.

He Thought He Knew What He Was Getting

A friend of mine detested fat women. He liked women who were thin. He wanted a wife who was thin. He avoided fat women. He avoided women whose mothers were fat. He wanted nothing to do with the genetics of fat parents, or women with heavy thighs or wide hips.

(I know this isn't "politically correct", but it's the way he thought.)

Finally he found a woman he considered marriage material. He watched her eating habits, he observed her mother's weight, and even made sure her sisters were all thin. Before getting married he had her promise she would never get fat.

And then she became fat.

After that he found he couldn't really have a good relationship with her because he hated the fact that he had married a woman who was NOT what he wanted.

In everything he had done it looked like his "vehicle" was pointed toward a thin woman. He WANTED thin, but in actuality his eyes were on "fat", and "fat" ended up being the abundance of his heart.

You can't pull "thin" out of your "bank account" when all you've deposited is "fat".

> *A good man out of the good treasure of his heart brings forth good things, and an evil man out of the evil treasure brings forth evil things.*
> – Matthew 12:35

When your vehicle is in reverse you have to be looking backward... your eyes are NOT going to be set in the direction your car is pointed. Your eyes will be set on where you're actually heading. Your eyes are predictors of your future.

> *Your eye is a lamp that provides light for your body. When your eye is good, your whole body is filled with light. But when it is bad, your body is filled with darkness. Make sure that the light you think you have is not actually darkness.*
> – Luke 11:34-35

This is another way of saying, "Your thoughts are seeds."

Thoughts are the seeds that grow up and produce your future. Whatever your thoughts are fixed on, negative or positive, actually predicts your future.

The WHY Matters

You *should* have a list of the qualities you want in the person you marry. It might be a mental list (like mine was) or a physical list (like the one my wife had). You should have a list because it will help you recognize those who might be a good fit. It will help you avoid settling for "second best".

> *It's not hard to make decisions when you know what your values are.*
> *– Unknown*

If you just want someone who "makes you feel loved", any number of people can do that. Not all of them are suitable for a long-term relationship.

Also, ask yourself why you want to "feel loved". Is it because you fear a life without love? Based on what we've covered in this chapter, you may very well end up with something other than what you THINK you want. Your "real" motives are likely to produce exactly what you DON'T want.

Before you put that item on your list it might be beneficial if you explore your own self-worth.

If you are looking for someone to build you up and make you feel worthwhile, I submit that you are "barking up the wrong tree". No person can consistently feed you what you need so you constantly feel worthwhile. YOU are actually the one who is responsible for that. If YOU are failing at that task, why should you expect anyone else to be successful at it?

✦ Things to Consider ✦

- Do you fear being alone in life? Learn to be comfortable with time alone... overcome your fear, or fear could bring what you least want.

- Be honest with yourself. Examine the motives behind what you "want". Spending time finding the truth now will help you avoid heartaches later.

- Realize you will be the answer to someone else's desires. What are they attracting to themselves when they attract you into their life?

- Like faith can attract the things you want, fear can attract the things you don't want. Faith and fear act the same... one is positive and produces positive results; the other is negative and produces negative results.

"For the thing which I greatly feared is come upon me, and that which I was afraid of is come unto me. I was not in safety, neither had I rest, neither was I quiet; yet trouble came."
– Job 3:26 (KJV)

A New Dimension of Prayer

> *What would you be willing to
> do to get God's help in praying
> out His perfect will for your life
> and those for whom you pray?*

Many of the answers to prayer I've experienced, including when I sought His will for my marriage, were obtained after sessions of praying in tongues.

What is this all about?

Receiving the Baptism in the Holy Spirit (with the ability to "speak in tongues") is the open door toward demonstrating the reality of Jesus' resurrection... in that He is still alive, and He still does the same things He did when He walked the earth.

Jesus said He wasn't the one working miracles, it was God the Father who did the works. BUT... Jesus did no miracles until the Holy Spirit came UPON Him. Jesus... the Son of God... with the life of God on the inside... for 30 years... but not working ANY miracles UNTIL AFTER the Holy Spirit came upon Him... and stayed.

The disciples had seen the resurrected Jesus, believed God had raised Him from the dead, and had confessed him as Lord. These are the ingredients to salvation, when one is "born again" and sealed with the Holy Spirit living within.

> *...if you confess with your mouth the Lord Jesus and believe in your heart that God has raised Him from the dead, you will be saved. For with the*

> *heart one believes unto righteousness, and with the mouth confession is made unto salvation.*
> — Romans 10:9-10

Then, in the very first chapter of Acts, Jesus instructs his disciples to WAIT until they received POWER from on high.

> *And being assembled together with [them], He commanded them not to depart from Jerusalem, but to wait for the Promise of the Father, "which," [He said], "you have heard from Me; for John truly baptized with water, but you shall be baptized with the Holy Spirit not many days from now.*
> — Acts 1:4-5

After that, in the upper room, during prayer, behind closed doors, the Holy Spirit came UPON each one of them.

> *When the Day of Pentecost had fully come, they were all with one accord in one place. And suddenly there came a sound from heaven, as of a rushing mighty wind, and it filled the whole house where they were sitting. Then there appeared to them divided tongues, as of fire, and [one] sat UPON each of them. And they were all filled with the Holy Spirit and began to speak with other tongues, as the Spirit gave them utterance [words to say].* — Acts 2:1-4

Notice... they already had the Spirit WITHIN, but needed the Spirit UPON to be able to DO THE WORKS. Just like Jesus, at the River Jordan... He had the Spirit WITHIN, but needed the Spirit UPON to DO THE WORKS.

My Experience

Realize that this is a GOOD thing. But like anything else, it's a choice.

God gives us the right to choose. He will not force anything on us, even when it's something good for us (like, for instance, Salvation).

> *If you then, being evil, know how to give good gifts to your children, how much more will [your] heavenly Father give the Holy Spirit to* **those who ask Him***!*
>
> *– Jesus (Luke 11:13)*

One of the hardest things I've ever done in my life was to yield to the Holy Spirit when I *asked* God to baptize me with the Holy Spirit.

I am the kind of person who likes to be in control... so to yield control to another, and to begin speaking out the non-sensical syllables that rose up within me, was hard. At the time I couldn't "speak in tongues" any louder than a whisper.

The minister who was helping me receive this new experience then gave me the best possible advice... "Go home and practice."

Supernatural Languages

I did. I went home and practiced.

I began to learn how to yield to the Spirit of God. As I devoted some time every day to "speaking in tongues" I began to progress beyond the whisper and on to praying in tongues in a normal voice. I then progressed to singing in tongues... and more. At one point I asked the Holy Spirit to help me move to new levels... to a broader "language"... and He was faithful as I stepped out in growing faith.

Since that time, during prayer meetings, or when I've prayed for others, I've had people tell me they understood the words I prayed when I was "speaking in tongues". To me the words that came out of me were unintelligible, but the hearers have heard complete sentences (and even paragraphs) in Haitian Creole, and in Japanese, and in Polish, and in Spanish.

(During one prayer session a missionary from Honduras had to move away from me because "Jayce was praying so much Spanish I couldn't focus on my own prayers.")

I don't know any of the above languages, yet the Holy Spirit knows them all. I spoke those languages because I had learned to YIELD to His leading.

Why pray in tongues?

When we pray in tongues the Holy Spirit helps us pray the perfect will of God... and we all need help in that. We don't see all the things that affect the situations we're praying for... all we can see is the information we can gather through our five senses. This is why the Bible says we don't know "what to pray for as (we) ought."

> *"Likewise the Spirit also helps in our [inability to produce results]. For we do not know what we should pray for as we ought, but the Spirit Himself makes intercession for us with groanings which cannot be uttered. Now He who searches the hearts knows what the mind of the Spirit [is], because He makes intercession for the saints according to [the will of] God."*
>
> – Romans 8:26,27

Why wouldn't anyone want to have the help of the Holy Spirit in prayer... knowing that He sees things we don't see... and that He knows the perfect will of God for our lives (and those for whom we are praying)... and He knows how to get answers. When one can actually get the help of God to pray the perfect will of God, that's amazing.

> *"I thank my God I speak with tongues more than you all;"*
> *– the Apostle Paul (*1 Corinthians 14:18*)*

And to think... I was initially afraid to step over into this amazing help.

Can you get answers from God without praying in tongues? I'm sure you can... but I wouldn't want to try it any other way.

If you've received this gift from God, I urge you to apply it when seeking His counsel.

If you haven't, I urge you to ask Him for the gift.

✦ Things to Consider ✦

- "... the Spirit helps us in our weakness (our inability to produce results). We do not know what we ought to pray for, **but the Spirit himself intercedes for us**..." – Romans 8:26

- "... the Spirit intercedes for the saints **in accordance with God's will**." – Romans 8:27

- "And **pray in the Spirit** on all occasions with all kinds of prayers and requests..." – Ephesians 6:18

- "... if **I pray in tongues, my spirit is praying**, but I don't understand what I am saying. Well then, what shall I do? **I will pray in the spirit**, and **I will also pray in words I understand**. I will sing in the spirit, and I will also sing in words I understand." – 1 Corinthians 14:14

*"Now we have received, not the spirit of the world, but the Spirit who is from God, **that we might know** the things that have been freely given to us by God."*

– 1 Corinthians 12:2

Thoughts about Marriage

Any couple can have a good marriage, IF they do the right things to MAKE it a good marriage.

Through the years I've gotten away from the concept that God has only one person who is right for you. That kind of theology just opens the door for hurt when the "one person" God planned for you to marry ends up "making a mistake" and marrying someone else. There are all kinds of religious thoughts and extremes that will then attempt to govern what should happen next...

- Stay single the rest of your life
- The person who made the mistake should divorce their mate and marry you
- And more outlandish ideas that bring more and more hurt to those involved

Personally, I like this philosophy:

Any couple can have a good marriage, IF they do the right things to MAKE it a good marriage.

Sadly, even many who were "right" for each other have experienced horrible marriages because they didn't do the things that make a good marriage.

Parallel Callings

The New Testament teaches that God has a purpose for each individual.

I believe anyone seeking a life-time relationship should first understand God's life purpose for their *own* life.

We taught our children that God has a plan and a destiny for each individual's life, and each person will most enjoy life when they're doing what they were made to do. We were fortunate that our children grew up in a church whose pastor was "destiny minded". Our children heard it at home AND from the pulpit. Very early in life they began to grasp the general direction God had for each of them, and that has been a huge foundation on which their life decisions are made.

I was not so fortunate. It wasn't until after I was saved that I began to catch a glimpse of the call on my life. Until then I bounced around with no real purpose.

How do I Find My Purpose?

Finding your purpose in life comes through the same advice I provided in the first two chapters of this book. The more time you spend with God, allowing Him to talk to you through the scriptures, the more you will see who He made you to be.

When you begin to recognize a purpose for your life you will want someone whose purpose and direction (and hopes and dreams) in life will run parallel to yours.

You don't want to be in a long-term relationship with one whose purpose and direction in life is divergent from yours. You would be foolish to choose someone whose inward pull is in a divergent direction from yours. Doing so would be a recipe for difficulty, conflict, unhappiness, and probable disaster.

✦ Things to Consider ✦

- Just because you find a "good fit" doesn't mean everything will go smoothly.

- Don't expect to marry a "finished product". You aren't perfect... Why should you expect your spouse to be perfect?

- Neither of you will be the same person 20 years from now. Expect each of you to change.

- When you have found one with a parallel life purpose, work to keep your interests compatible.

- Invest time, attention and consideration into each other.

- Remember, YOU are the only person you can change. Recognize the majority of your problems stem from who YOU are... what *your* heart is full of.

*And do not be conformed to this world, but be transformed by the renewing of your mind, that you may prove what [is] that good and acceptable and perfect will of God, **even the thing which is good and acceptable and perfect [in His sight for you]**.*

– Romans 12:2
(combining NKJV & Amplified versions)

References

1. The Jewish Encyclopedia: Urim and Thummim (http://www.jewishencyclopedia.com/articles/14609-urim-and-thummim)

2. "and the peace of God, which surpasses all understanding, will guard your hearts and minds through Christ Jesus." – Philemon 4:7

3. "Do not be deceived, God is not mocked; for whatever a man sows, that he will also reap." – Galatians 6:7

Please Post a Review

Did this book help you? Please consider posting a review for the book on Amazon.com.

Book Store Orders

For book store discounts, please use the contact form at http://tohline.com/contact/

More Articles

More articles and books by Jayce Tohline can be found at http://tohline.com/

Contact Information

Jayce Tohline has been called a "spiritual technician". The term fits because he enjoys the process of learning, finding out how things work, proving it out in his own life, and then sharing that knowledge with others. He often approaches truths from a "different side of the mountain" than what is generally heard from the pulpit. But his approach allows others to easily understand spiritual principles and how to put them to work successfully in their own lives.

His desire is to help people reach their full, God-given potential. He specializes in the practical application of scripture (the Word of God) to the individual's every-day life.

Speaking Engagements

Contact Jayce Tohline through the contact form at http://tohline.com/contact/

Made in the USA
Middletown, DE
18 February 2016